Good Neighbours

The New East Enders Series

Written by Marta Paluch

Illustrated by Mary Pierce

Good Neighbours
Text copyright © Marta Paluch 2014
Illustrations copyright © Mary Pierce 2014

Published in 2014 by Gatehouse Media Limited

ISBN: 978-1-84231-091-5

British Library Cataloguing-in-Publication Data:
A catalogue record for this book is available from the British Library

**ESSEX COUNTY
COUNCIL LIBRARY**

No part of this publication may be reproduced in any form or by any means, electronic, mechanical, photocopying, recording or otherwise, without the prior written consent of the publishers.

Authors' Note

In 2003 the ESOL Outreach team at Tower Hamlets College gained funding from the East London ESOL Pathfinder to produce a pack of teaching materials relevant to the context of Outreach ESOL classes. Tower Hamlets College was the lead partner for the East London ESOL Pathfinder.

The resulting pack of materials included 6 easy reading booklets for beginning ESOL learners. The reading booklets proved popular and it was suggested that we should try to get them published. We approached Avantibooks who agreed to publish them as a series entitled *The New Eastenders*, but those books are now out of print.

We are delighted that they have now been given a new lease of life by Gatehouse Books as *The New East Enders Series* for a new generation of ESOL learners. We have added a seventh title to the series, called *My Mother-in-Law*, and a useful set of tutor resources and student worksheets. We hope you enjoy using them.

Marta Paluch & Mary Pierce

This is Amina.
She is 35 years old.
She's married.

This is Amina's family.

This is Ahmed.
He is Amina's husband.
He's 38 years old.
He's a chef in a restaurant.

This is Yusuf.
He is Amina's son.
He's 13 years old.
He's a student at Saint Paul's Way School.

This is Samira.
She is Amina's daughter.
She's 10 years old.
She's a pupil at Marner School.

This is Asia.
She is Samira's sister.
She's 6 years old.
She's a pupil at Marner School.

This is Hassan.
He is Amina's baby.
He's 10 months old.
He's at home with Amina.

This is Amina's home.
It's a council flat.
It's in Bow. It's a nice flat.
Amina is happy.

This is Fadumo and her family.
They are Amina's neighbours.
They're from Somalia.

Fadumo's husband is in Somalia.
Fadumo is in London with her children.
This is difficult.
Fadumo isn't happy.

This is Ibrahim. He is Fadumo's son.
He's 14 years old.
He is Yusuf's friend.
They are in the same class at school.

This is Saint Paul's Way School.
It's a big school.
The students are noisy.

This is Zahra.
She's Fadumo's daughter.
She's 8 years old.
She's a pupil at Marner School.

This is David Jones.
He's Zahra's teacher.
He's a nice teacher.
Zahra is happy at school.

Amina's family and Fadumo's family are friends.
Fadumo and Zahra are in Amina's house.
Ibrahim and Yusuf are outside.
The two families are good neighbours.

If you have enjoyed this book, why not try one of these other titles from *The New East Enders Series:*

A New Home
Fadumo Goes Shopping
From Here to There
My Mother-in-Law
My Son is Sick
Rima's Day

A comprehensive set of tutor resources is available to support this series of readers:

**The New East Enders Series
Tutor Resources CD-ROM**

ISBN: 978-1-84231-094-6